The Sensory Coach's
A Year and a Day of Gratitude

"Begin your day with gratitude and end your day with gratitude. A heart filled with loving expressions of thanks is a beautiful offering to the universe."

~ Susan Barbara Apollon ~

All rights reserved. No part of this book may be reproduced or transmitted in any form by any means, electronic or mechanical, including photocopying, scanning and recording, or by any information storage and retrieval system, without permission in writing from the publisher, except for the review for inclusion in a magazine, newspaper or broadcast.

Copyright © 2021 Techla Wood

take the FREE Sensory Types Quiz at:
WWW.THESENSORYCOACH.COM/SENSORY-TYPES-QUIZ/

This Gratitude Journal belongs to:

____

THE BENEFITS OF GRATITUDE JOURNALLING

Looking for things to be grateful for can feel like an impossible task when we're having a bad day, week, month or even year. However, plumbing the depths of our days to find even one thing to be grateful for, can have enormous benefits for our health and wellbeing, with the knock-on effects rippling out into the wider world.

Gratitude focuses our attention on the here and now - what is already in our life that we are grateful for?

Gratitude, when practised regularly, can help ease depression. It can increase feelings of joy, happiness, contentedness and appreciation as well our increasing our sense of connection with our surroundings and the people in our lives.

As with any practice, gratitude is something that is best done regularly. A daily practice is the ideal, but in our busy lives, this can sometimes feel like one more impossible thing to commit to.

That's why I've made sure to keep the daily entry spaces short and sweet. There's nothing to stop you from making long and detailed journal entries in another space, but this journal is for capturing the essence of the moment you are grateful for.

It's a space that you will be able to easily flick through in the months ahead and be reminded quickly of all the good that you have in your life.

There are many different ways to go about this practice such as:

- list 3 things you are grateful for each day

- choose one thing to focus your gratitude on and write about it at the end of the day
- commit to a random act of kindness and write about it
- Send loving thoughts to someone in your life and use the space to write about why you're grateful for them
- Show your appreciation for a stranger by thanking them for their help, or simply sharing a smile with them - write about how it made you feel
- Look around you and cast your eyes on something that brings you pleasure - write about what it adds to your life
- Write about something in the natural world that brightens your day

I'm sure you'll think of a thousand and one different ways you can express gratitude for the wonders, big and small, that you experience each and every day.

If you get stuck, just look through the encouraging quotes that are at the bottom of every page, they're sure to inspire you.

Whatever you choose to be grateful for, make sure you make an entry in your journal every day, so that before you know, this has become a practice that you look forward to. With each new entry, you're creating a more joyful life, not just for you but for everyone you come into contact with. Gratitude and joyfulness are contagious, so let's spread them far and wide!

Date   /   /

Date   /   /

Date   /   /

"Let us be grateful to the people who make us happy; they are the charming gardeners who make our souls blossom."

~ Marcel Proust ~

Date   /   /

Date   /   /

Date   /   /

"Be mindful. Be grateful. Be positive. Be true. Be kind."

~ Roy T. Bennett ~

Date   /   /

Date   /   /

Date   /   /

"Walk as if you are kissing the Earth with your feet."
~ Thich Nhat Hanh ~

Date   /   /

Date   /   /

Date   /   /

"Do not spoil what you have by desiring what you have not; remember that what
you now have was once among the things you only hoped for."
~ Epicurus ~

Date   /   /

Date   /   /

Date   /   /

"We can complain because rose bushes have thorns, or rejoice because thorns have

roses."

~ Alphonse Karr ~

Date   /   /

Date   /   /

Date   /   /

"Sometimes life knocks you on your ass… get up, get up, get up!!! Happiness
is not the absence of problems, it's the ability to deal with them."
~ Steve Maraboli ~

Date   /   /

Date   /   /

Date   /   /

"Piglet noticed that even though he had a Very Small Heart, it could hold a rather large amount of Gratitude."

~ A.A. Milne ~

Date   /   /

Date   /   /

Date   /   /

"Cultivate the habit of being grateful for every good thing that comes to you, and to give thanks continuously. And because all things have contributed to your advancement, you should include all things in your gratitude."
~ Ralph Waldo Emerson ~

Date   /   /

Date   /   /

Date   /   /

*"Acknowledging the good that you already have in your life is the foundation
for all abundance."*

~ Eckhart Tolle ~

Date   /   /

Date   /   /

Date   /   /

""Let gratitude be the pillow upon which you kneel to say your nightly prayer.
And let faith be the bridge you build to overcome evil and welcome good."
~ Maya Angelou ~

Date   /   /

Date   /   /

Date   /   /

"If the only prayer you said was thank you, that would be enough."
~ Meister Eckhart ~

Date   /   /

Date   /   /

Date   /   /

"You pray in your distress and in your need; would that you might pray also in the fullness of your joy and in your days of abundance."
~ Kahill Gibran ~

Date   /   /

Date   /   /

Date   /   /

"We must find time to stop and thank the people who make a difference in our lives."

~ John F. Kennedy ~

Date   /   /

Date   /   /

Date   /   /

"If having a soul means being able to feel love and loyalty and gratitude, then
animals are better off than a lot of humans."

~ James Herriot ~

Date   /   /

Date   /   /

Date   /   /

"Gratitude is not only the greatest of virtues, but the parent of all others."
~ Marcus Tullius Cicero ~

Date   /   /

Date   /   /

Date   /   /

"Appreciation is a wonderful thing. It makes what is excellent in others belong
to us as well."

~ Voltaire ~

Date   /   /

Date   /   /

Date   /   /

"When you are grateful, fear disappears and abundance appears."
~ Anthony Robbins ~

Date   /   /

Date   /   /

Date   /   /

"In normal life we hardly realize how much more we receive than we give, and life cannot be rich without such gratitude. It is so easy to overestimate the importance of our own achievements compared with what we owe to the help of others."

~ Dietrich Bonhoeffer ~

Date   /   /

Date   /   /

Date   /   /

"The unthankful heart discovers no mercies; but the thankful heart will find,
in every hour, some heavenly blessings."
~ Henry Ward Beecher ~

Date   /   /

Date   /   /

Date   /   /

"We should certainly count our blessings, but we should also make our
blessings count."
~ Neal A. Maxwell ~

Date   /   /

Date   /   /

Date   /   /

"It's a funny thing about life, once you begin to take note of the things you are
grateful for, you begin to lose sight of the things that you lack."
~ Germany Kent ~

Date   /   /

Date   /   /

Date   /   /

"What separates privilege from entitlement is gratitude."

~ Brené Brown ~

Date   /   /

Date   /   /

Date   /   /

"Got no checkbooks, got no banks. Still I'd like to express my thanks — I've got the sun in the mornin' and the moon at night."

~ Irving Berlin ~

Date   /   /

Date   /   /

Date   /   /

"There is strange comfort in knowing that no matter what happens today, the
Sun will rise again tomorrow."
~ Aaron Lauritsen ~

Date   /   /

Date   /   /

Date   /   /

"Breath is the finest gift of nature. Be grateful for this wonderful gift."

~ Amit Ray ~

Date   /   /

Date   /   /

Date   /   /

"The most beautiful moments in life are moments when you are expressing your joy, not when you are seeking it."

~ Jaggi Vasudev ~

Date   /   /

Date   /   /

Date   /   /

"Whatever you appreciate and give thanks for will increase in your life."
~ Sanaya Roman ~

Date   /   /

Date   /   /

Date   /   /

"Regardless of Sunshine or Rain, Be Thankful for another GREAT day...and treat Life as the ULTIMATE Gift.... Because IT IS :)"

~ Pablo ~

Date   /   /

Date   /   /

Date   /   /

"I think that real friendship always makes us feel such sweet gratitude, because the world almost always seems like a very hard desert, and the flowers that grow there seem to grow against such high odds."

~ Stephen King ~

Date   /   /

Date   /   /

Date   /   /

"Gratitude bestows reverence.....changing forever how we experience life and the world."

~ John Milton ~

Date   /   /

Date   /   /

Date   /   /

"When it comes to life the critical thing is whether you take things for granted
or take them with gratitude."

~ G.K. Chesterton ~

Date   /   /

Date   /   /

Date   /   /

"An attitude of gratitude brings great things."
~ Yogi Bhajan ~

Date   /   /

Date   /   /

Date   /   /

"Take full account of what Excellencies you possess, and in gratitude
remember how you would hanker after them, if you had them not."
~ Marcus Aurelius ~

Date   /   /

Date   /   /

Date   /   /

"I may not be where I want to be but I'm thankful for not being where I used to be."

~ Habeeb Akande ~

Date   /   /

Date   /   /

Date   /   /

"Gratitude is the ability to experience life as a gift. It liberates us from the prison of self-preoccupation."

~ John Ortberg ~

Date   /   /

Date   /   /

Date   /   /

"When you express gratitude for the blessings that come into your life, it not only encourages the universe to send you more, it also sees to it that those blessings remain."

~ Stephen Richards ~

Date   /   /

Date   /   /

Date   /   /

"If we want to keep the blessings of life coming to us, we must learn to be grateful for whatever is given."

~ Harold Klemp ~

Date   /   /

Date   /   /

Date   /   /

"It's up to us to choose contentment and thankfulness now—and to stop imagining that we have to have everything perfect before we'll be happy."

~ Joanna Gaines ~

Date   /   /

Date   /   /

Date   /   /

"Those who are not grateful soon begin to complain of everything."
~ Thomas Merton ~

Date   /   /

Date   /   /

Date   /   /

"Thankfulness creates gratitude which generates contentment that causes
peace."
~ Todd Stocker ~

Date   /   /

Date   /   /

Date   /   /

"A sincere attitude of gratitude is a beatitude for secured altitudes.
Appreciate what you have been given and you will be promoted higher."
~ Israelmore Ayivor ~

Date   /   /

Date   /   /

Date   /   /

"Gratitude helps you to grow and expand; gratitude brings JOY and laughter
into your life and into the lives of all those around you."

~ Eileen Caddy ~

Date   /   /

Date   /   /

Date   /   /

"Because gratitude is the key to happiness, anything that undermines gratitude must undermine happiness. And nothing undermines gratitude as much as expectations. There is an inverse relationship between expectations and gratitude: The more expectations you have, the less gratitude you will have."
~ Dennis Prager ~

Date   /   /

Date   /   /

Date   /   /

"Joy is the simplest form of gratitude."
~ Karl Barth ~

"Find magic in the little things, and the big things you always expected will start to show up."

~ Isa Zapata ~

Date   /   /

Date   /   /

Date   /   /

"Gratitude always comes into play, research shows that people are happier if they are grateful for the positive things in their lives, rather than worrying about what might be missing."
~ Dan Buettner ~

Date   /   /

Date   /   /

Date   /   /

"In every class of society, gratitude is the rarest of all human virtues."
~ Wilkie Collins ~

Date   /   /

Date   /   /

Date   /   /

"Most of us forget to take time for wonder, praise and gratitude until it is almost too late. Gratitude is a many-colored quality, reaching in all directions. It goes out for small things and for large; it is a God-ward going."
~ Faith Baldwin ~

Date   /   /

Date   /   /

Date   /   /

"Summoning gratitude is a sure way to get our life back on track. Opening our eyes to affirm gratitude grows the garden of our inner abundance, just as standing close to a fire eventually warms our heart."

~ Alexandra Katehakis ~

Date   /   /

Date   /   /

Date   /   /

"Gratitude and love are always multiplied when you give freely. It is an infinite source of contentment and prosperous energy."

~ Jim Fargiano ~

Date   /   /

Date   /   /

Date   /   /

"Saying thanks to the world, and acknowledging your own accomplishments, is a great way to feel good and stay positive."
~ Rachel Robins ~

Date   /   /

Date   /   /

Date   /   /

"Gratitude is an overflow of the pleasure filling your soul."
~ Raheel Farooq ~

Date   /   /

Date   /   /

Date   /   /

Date   /   /

Date   /   /

Date   /   /

"Express gratitude for the greatness of small things."
~ Richie Norton ~

Date   /   /

Date   /   /

Date   /   /

"Find gratitude in the little things and your well of gratitude will never run dry."

~ Antonia Montoya ~

Date   /   /

Date   /   /

Date   /   /

"The soul that gives thanks can find comfort in everything; the soul that complains can find comfort in nothing."

~ Hannah Whitall Smith ~

Date / /

Date / /

Date / /

"Expectation has brought me disappointment. Disappointment has brought me wisdom. Acceptance, gratitude and appreciation have brought me joy and fulfilment."

~ Rasheed Ogunlaru ~

Date   /   /

Date   /   /

Date   /   /

"Gratitude also opens your eyes to the limitless potential of the universe, while dissatisfaction closes your eyes to it."
~ Stephen Richards ~

Date   /   /

Date   /   /

Date   /   /

"Never let the things you want make you forget the things you have."
~ Sanchita Pandey ~

Date   /   /

Date   /   /

Date   /   /

"We can never bring anything to us unless we are grateful for what we have. In fact, if somebody were completely and utterly grateful for everything, they would never have to ask for anything, because it would be given to them before they even asked."

~ Rhonda Byrne ~

Date   /   /

Date   /   /

Date   /   /

"Count your blessings as the more you are grateful for what you have the more there is to be grateful for."

~ Pravin Agarwal ~

Date   /   /

Date   /   /

Date   /   /

"When you feel thankful, you can be appreciative for a moment, then not at all the next. It seems the tank is full, then it becomes empty, and the cycle continues. If you don't feel the same gratitude for a moment, know that it's possible in the next moment that comes around."

~ J.R. Rim ~

Date   /   /

Date   /   /

Date   /   /

Date   /   /

Date   /   /

Date   /   /

"Embrace every new day with gratitude, hope and love."
~ Lailah Gifty Akita ~

Date   /   /

Date   /   /

Date   /   /

"More Miracles occur from Gratitude and Forgiveness than anything else"
~ Philip H. Friedman ~

Date   /   /

Date   /   /

Date   /   /

"Rather than getting more spoilt with age, as difficulties pile up, epiphanies
of gratitude abound."
~ Alain de Botton ~

Date   /   /

Date   /   /

Date   /   /

"Be grateful for whatever it is that opens you up."

~ Allan G. Hunter ~

Date   /   /

Date   /   /

Date   /   /

"Grateful people are happy people. The more things you are grateful for, the happier you will be."

~ Roy T. Bennett ~

Date   /   /

Date   /   /

Date   /   /

"Ask. Trust. Give thanks. Simple right?"

~ Dawn Gluskin ~

Date   /   /

Date   /   /

Date   /   /

"Practicing gratitude is like turning the dimmer switch up. Things you never
noticed before keep lighting up your heart.
(They always were there, just unlit.)"
~ Kelly Corbet ~

Date   /   /

Date   /   /

Date   /   /

"Every time you feel gratitude, you're reminding your brain to look for more ways to be grateful. As you bask in noticing life's abundance, your body rewards you with serotonin, oxytocin and dopamine – boosting your immunity and energy."

~ Simona Ondrejkova ~

Date   /   /

Date   /   /

Date   /   /

"If you visit a garden in spring, don't focus on the prickles of a solitary rose."
~ Wayne Gerard Trotman ~

Date   /   /

Date   /   /

Date   /   /

"There are things I can never do again, people I can never see again, dreams I can never dream again. And yet I wake up every morning with a heart full of gratitude to be alive."

~ Marty Rubin ~

Date   /   /

Date   /   /

Date   /   /

"Gratitude is inherently selfless. It is unconditional and shows internal appreciation toward other people. Doing so can influence two critical processes in your life, namely catharsis, and reciprocity. Both of these responses are directly related to your happiness."

~ Robert Gill Jr. ~

Date   /   /

Date   /   /

Date   /   /

"Focus on what others have and you feel that you have so little.
Focus on what you do have and you realize that you have so much."
~ Hrishikesh Agnihotri ~

Date   /   /

Date   /   /

Date   /   /

"When pursuing happiness in life I focus on having gratitude"
~ Angel Moreira ~

Date   /   /

Date   /   /

Date   /   /

"It's a scientific fact that gratitude reciprocates."

~ Matthew McConaughey ~

Date   /   /

Date   /   /

Date   /   /

"Be silent as to services you have rendered, but speak of favours you have
received."

~ Seneca the Younger ~

Date   /   /

Date   /   /

Date   /   /

"There is something to appreciate in every moment of every day. Strive to find it as often as you can. Living with gratitude will change your life."
~ Anthon St. Maarten ~

Date   /   /

Date   /   /

Date   /   /

"Anything you can't be grateful for becomes your baggage. Anything that you
are grateful for becomes your fuel. Habituate gratitude"
~ Premlatha Rajkumar ~

Date   /   /

Date   /   /

Date   /   /

"She had gradually discovered that the best response to glorious, unexpected happiness was not to seek explanation for its appearance but simply to embrace it and be glad."
~ Janice Hadlow ~

Date   /   /

Date   /   /

Date   /   /

"Socrates reportedly said "The unexamined life is not worth living." While true, I believe that the unappreciated life - is no life at all. Every day we have a choice. We can color the snapshot in time with intention, joy and gratitude or we can let the picture fade to grey."
~ Evan Archerd ~

Date   /   /

Date   /   /

Date   /   /

"Gratitude produces happiness because it focuses your thoughts on the positive. And when you are in a positive mental attitude, you bring more good things to your life to be grateful for"

~ Caro Briones ~

Date   /   /

Date   /   /

Date   /   /

"One of the easiest ways to feel better off is to think what we have and have
gratitude for it"
~ Tonmoy Acharjee ~

Date   /   /

Date   /   /

Date   /   /

"There can't be joy until there is gratitude."
~ Melissa Ambrosini ~

Date   /   /

Date   /   /

Date   /   /

"Gratitude makes sweet miracles of small moments."

~ Mary Davis ~

Date   /   /

Date   /   /

Date   /   /

"Feeling is being alive... let's feel another day to live another day and lets choose the first feeling of every day to be grateful of this beautifully precious life that we are blessed to have."

~ Judy Phin ~

Date   /   /

Date   /   /

Date   /   /

"In pursuing our passions, following our hearts, and believing that life, and the people in the world, are mostly good, choosing gratitude and joy becomes second nature to us."

~ Mary Potter Kenyon ~

Date   /   /

Date   /   /

Date   /   /

"Grant me daily the grace of gratitude, to be thankful for all my gifts, and so
be freed from artificial needs, that I might lead a joyful, simple life."
~ Edward Hays ~

Date   /   /

Date   /   /

Date   /   /

"It's okay to find gratitude in solitude."
~ Lidia Longorio ~

Date   /   /

Date   /   /

Date   /   /

"Don't Lament For What You Couldn't Do. Instead, Celebrate With
Gratitude, For What You Could"."
~ Venugopal Acharya ~

Date   /   /

Date   /   /

Date   /   /

"Gratitude is strongly and consistently associated with greater happiness.
Gratitude helps people feel more positive emotions, relish good experiences,
improve their health, deal with adversity, and build strong relationships."
~ Abhishek Ratna ~

Date   /   /

Date   /   /

Date   /   /

"The true poetic feeling is one of boundless gratitude."
~ Marty Rubin ~

Date   /   /

Date   /   /

Date   /   /

Date   /   /

Date   /   /

Date   /   /

""gratitude makes people take a step back and see the value of what they have and thereby appreciate it more, which makes it less likely that they take it for granted."
~ Meik Wiking ~

Date   /   /

Date   /   /

Date   /   /

"Gratitude is what turns what may seem as an intensely painful life into an
intensely thrilling adventure."
~ Itayi Garande ~

Date   /   /

Date   /   /

Date   /   /

"Grateful people generate a higher vibration, and a stronger energy because they run on love and awareness that life is a true gift."

~ Toni Sorenson ~

Date   /   /

Date   /   /

Date   /   /

"Every time we decide to be grateful it will be easier to see new things to be grateful for. Gratitude begets gratitude, just as love begets love."

~ Henri J. M. Nouwen ~

Date   /   /

Date   /   /

Date   /   /

"By allowing myself to just be, i give myself space to purr in gratitude. I am the observer. I allow myself the time and space I need."

~ Petra Poje ~

Date   /   /

Date   /   /

Date   /   /

"Live a life full of humility, gratitude, intellectual curiosity, and never stop
learning."
~ Gza ~

Date   /   /

Date   /   /

Date   /   /

"We are most ourselves, the most human, when we unabashedly immerse ourselves in the world with love and hope, gratitude and kindness."

~ John Sean Doyle ~

Date   /   /

Date   /   /

Date   /   /

"Gratitude is a feedback loop that will show you where you are thriving."
~ Danielle LaPorte ~

Date   /   /

Date   /   /

Date   /   /

"Before you get mad of someone, find something he \she did for you that
deserve gratitude"
~ Asmaa Dokmak ~

Date   /   /

Date   /   /

Date   /   /

""Gratitude is the foundation of compassion."

~ Master Jun Hong Lu ~

Date   /   /

Date   /   /

Date   /   /

"We have so many things to be grateful for, if only we took a moment to appreciate them."

~ Sai Pradeep ~

Date   /   /

Date   /   /

Date   /   /

"If life is a cup of tea, gratitude is the honey that makes it sweet."
~ Natasha Potter ~

Date   /   /

Date   /   /

Date   /   /

"If you fail to carry around with you a heart of gratitude for the love you've been so freely given, it is easy for you not to love others as you should."

~ Paul David Tripp ~

Date   /   /

Date   /   /

Date   /   /

"When I force myself to utter the awkward phrase, "I am grateful," I actually start to feel a bit more grateful... It's basic cognitive behavioral therapy: Behave in a certain way, and your mind will eventually catch up with your actions."

~ A.J. Jacobs ~

Date   /   /

Date   /   /

Date   /   /

""Nothing feels better than the privilege of being alive. Be grateful for life.
Not everyone made it thus far."
~ Gift Gugu Mona ~

Date   /   /

Date   /   /

Date   /   /

"The simple act of practicing gratitude, consistently, is your invitation to a new life. Accepting the invitation is now up to you."

~ Josie Robinson ~

Date   /   /

Date   /   /

Date   /   /

"You can't fix everything. Not even close. But you can look for reasons to be grateful. More than that, you can work to create them."

~ Katherine Center ~

Date   /   /

Date   /   /

Date   /   /

Date   /   /

Date   /   /

Date   /   /

"There is always something to be #grateful for. Take time to reflect and
appreciate what you have"
~ Rosalie Bardo ~

Date   /   /

Date   /   /

Date   /   /

Date   /   /

Date   /   /

Date   /   /

"A major component of health and wellness, gratitude helps us to appreciate the blessings we already have and sparks the anticipatory pleasure of blessings to come."

~ Laurie Buchanan, PhD ~

Date   /   /

Date   /   /

Date   /   /

"With a highly developed attitude of gratitude, we truly multiply how much love and joy we feel towards everyone we have known."

~ Michael Mirdad ~

Date   /   /

Date   /   /

Date   /   /

"Gratitude, opens my eyes and my heart to the many, many blessings in my life."

~ Maria Defillo ~

Date   /   /

Date   /   /

Date   /   /

"A path toward self-realization necessarily demands gratitude."

— Joseph Rain

Date   /   /

Date   /   /

Date   /   /

"Negativity is contagious, gratitude is the antidote."
~ Connie C. Perez ~

Date   /   /

Date   /   /

Date   /   /

"Without gratitude, we can't appreciate all the gifts that life gives us every day."
~ Avina Celeste ~

Date   /   /

Date   /   /

Date   /   /

"If you are not grateful for what you have, how do you know that you will be grateful for the thing that you are longing for?"

~ Jeremiah Browne ~

Date   /   /

Date   /   /

Date   /   /

"Gratitude possesses all the energy of a sunbeam. That is how it makes life blossom."

~ Richelle E. Goodrich ~

www.ingramcontent.com/pod-product-compliance
Lightning Source LLC
Chambersburg PA
CBHW051428150726
48000CB00005B/1997